W9-BKF-935

STOMPIN' AT THE SAVOY

STOMPIN'
AT THE SAVOY
THE STORY OF NORMA MILLER

collected and edited by ALAN GOVENAR

illustrated by MARTIN FRENCH

CANDLEWICK PRESS
CAMBRIDGE, MASSACHUSETTS

In memory of swing dancers lost along the way
N. M. and A. G.

In memory of Lena Franchetti
M. F.

Text copyright © 2006 by Alan Govenar and Norma Miller
Illustrations copyright © 2006 by Martin French

All rights reserved. No part of this book may be reproduced, transmitted,
or stored in an information retrieval system in any form or by any means,
graphic, electronic, or mechanical, including photocopying, taping,
and recording, without prior written permission from the publisher.

Library of Congress Cataloging-in-Publication Data
Miller, Norma, 1919–.
Stompin' at the Savoy : the story of Norma Miller / collected and edited
by Alan Govenar ; illustrated by Martin French
p. cm.
First-person account of the life of Norma Miller.
ISBN 0-7636-2244-3
1. Miller, Norma, 1919– —Juvenile literature. 2. Women dancers—United States—
Biography—Juvenile literature. I. Govenar, Alan B., date. II. French, Martin, ill. III. Title.
GV1785.M522A3 2006
792.8'092—dc22
[B]   2004057916

2 4 6 8 10 9 7 5 3 1

Printed in the United States of America

This book was typeset in Berkeley OldStyle.
The illustrations were done in ink, acrylic, graphite,
and charcoal on paper, and digitally.

Candlewick Press
2067 Massachusetts Avenue
Cambridge, Massachusetts 02140

visit us at www.candlewick.com

*It don't mean a thing
if it ain't got that swing.*

DUKE ELLINGTON, IRVIN MILLS

To talk with Norma Miller is to swing-step into the past. Jazz dance is her life, and this book is a portrait of her growing up and coming of age, based on a series of conversations we started in the spring of 2001. I was working on a new musical, now entitled *Blind Lemon Blues,* in collaboration with Akin Babatunde, and Norma agreed to come to Dallas to teach dance steps of the 1920s to the cast.

Norma liked to reminisce, and as I listened, I was drawn into her stories as if they had happened just days or weeks before. Her memories were at once detailed and honed with an unpretentious humor. She liked to joke about herself but never seemed to exaggerate.

A few months later, I met up with Norma in New York. She was wearing a hot-pink sweatsuit, a sequined cap, and a red leather jacket. She was standing majestically in front of the Carlyle Hotel, at 76th Street and Madison Avenue, and she chuckled as I walked toward her. On the sidewalks of New York, Norma had a natural grace. She was relaxed but acutely aware. She had an uncanny ability to evoke a sense of people, places, and events, as if she were taking me into her past as her guest.

The next time I saw Norma in New York, we went to Luci's, on 124th Street and Eighth Avenue, where the fifteen-piece Harlem Renaissance Orchestra started up around nine-thirty.

"The dancers gather here every Monday," Norma said. "It's a place to meet up with people I've known for more than fifty years and to get to know others I've never met before."

While we looked on, two young Japanese women wearing circle skirts, bobby socks, and black-and-white soft-soled shoes took the dance floor with two African American men who were probably old enough to be their grandparents, seasoned veterans of the swing-dance era. One, Calvin, had a ballroom grace, and, as Norma explained, "He swings it." Each gesture of his hands and feet moved fluidly. His young partner followed his lead as he spun her out and pulled her back in. Norma leaned back, confident that the Lindy Hop was indeed passing from one generation to the next, and closed her eyes, deep in the swing beat of Basie's "Jumpin' at the Woodside."

For Norma, so much of the beauty of life is what happens as each day unfolds. She embraces the moment but never loses sight of who she is or where she came from. She has a clear sense of the past and a passionate vision of the promise tomorrow may bring. In working with her to make this book, I tape-recorded and tran-scribed our ongoing dialogue. Each time we talked, we refined the process. The book embodies the sound and spirit of Norma's voice, collected into a series of chapters that chronicle her early years and coming of age. Through my editing, I strove to re-create the point of view of hearing and experiencing these stories as Norma told them for the first time.

My Father Disappears

My mother was eight months pregnant with me when my father died. My father was coming home from work one day, and some men from the U.S. Army took him off the street. He was from the West Indies, and Mama said that was the way they recruited immigrants back then. They took all the black men coming up out of the subway and spirited them away on a truck and put them in the army. They made him go to work in the New York City shipyards on one of those big battleships, and he caught pneumonia.

My mother went to see him in the hospital. "Do we have any money?" she asked him. "Do you have any papers? Do you have any insurance?" He just lay back on his pillow and shook his head, smiling. In those days, they didn't have penicillin, and he got sicker.

I've always said my father died laughing. In tragedy, we had to find some humor. Tears never came. Laughter was our means to survive.

There was no insurance and no money to bury him. So they buried my father with other soldiers in a potter's field, a cemetery for paupers. I was never told where it was, and I never asked. More than likely, it was somewhere in Brooklyn. Who kept up with graves in those days?

My father died in November, and I was born on December 2, 1919. My mother called me Norma after him. His name was Norman.

WHAT IS MAMA GOING TO DO?

My mother was twenty years old, had two children, no husband, and could barely find a job. So she went to talk to the priest at St. Philip's, the Episcopalian church between Seventh and Eighth Avenues on 134th Street. St. Philip's was a church where a lot of the West Indians went. My sister and I were christened there.

The priest at St. Philip's advised Mama to take my sister, Dot, and me to a home, basically an orphanage, where we could stay until she got stabilized. When she took us over there, the home said they would take Dot, who was almost two, but not me, because I was still a babe in Mama's arms.

While my mother was standing there talking to the people in charge, a little girl pulled the hem of her skirt and asked, "Are you my mama?" My mother looked down and shook her head. She swore to herself, "This will never happen to us." She would suck salt before she would ever separate herself from her children. And from then on, she scuffled around to make a living.

Mama used to say, "When you ain't got a horse, you ride a cow." That was always our philosophy, and with that, we survived, some kind of way.

My mother put bread on the table. She was the king of the house. She worked all the time. And like she always said, she worked so I could have long fingernails. And that's why I've always had long fingernails.

House-Rent Parties

To help pay the rent, Mama used to hold house-rent parties. Everyone who squeezed into our small apartment paid twenty-five cents to listen to music and dance. Mama served pigs' feet, potato salad, and souse (a thick sauce made from cucumber, celery, vinegar, lemon, and cayenne pepper).

At house-rent parties, which we usually had about once a month, there were no bands. There'd be a wind-up Victrola, and sometimes an upright piano. Somebody'd play ragtime, or what we called stride. It was music that made people want to dance.

The parties often started late at night. I would sleep

under the coats in the bedroom, but when I heard the words "ice cream," I'd get up and dance for some. I loved to do the Charleston, and everyone thought I was a champ.

"She's going to be a star!" they'd say.

I don't know where the Charleston came from. I just saw people doing it, and I did it. The Charleston was the rage of the 1920s.

Dancing was a major part of everything we did. Everything was jazz in those days: syncopated rhythms and dance. It was the Jazz Age, and Harlem was the center of it all.

THE LITTLE BLACKBIRD

I was five years old when I saw Florence Mills perform at the Lincoln Theatre, on 135th Street between Lenox and Fifth Avenues. She was known as the Little Blackbird and was the first big star I was aware of in Harlem. She was a dancer and star of Lew Leslie's *Blackbirds*. I wanted to be just like her.

Florence Mills went to Europe in 1926 and was a sensation. But while she was there, she fell ill, and she died soon after she came home to New York. I was almost eight. Her funeral was the biggest public spectacle I had ever seen. I followed the hearse down Seventh Avenue, and they released a flock of blackbirds that flew through the sky above the procession.

DANCE SCHOOL

I was nine or ten years old when Mama enrolled me at Amanda Kemp's dance school. It cost twenty-five cents an hour, and we could barely afford that. All the kids in my neighborhood went to some kind of dancing school. And after dance class, I went looking for the new stage shows, the musicals and the revues, because all the shows rehearsed in Harlem.

In those days, everybody who wanted to put together a show came to New York, because New York had theaters, and these entrepreneurs would bring the shows to rehearsal halls in Harlem. You could go to any of them, and there would be some show rehearsing. You always heard a piano tinkling. People were dancing. Tap dancers were off in the corner. I used to go there and watch. I'd stand off to the side and look in the door. I watched the routines and watched them dance. And when I'd come out, I'd know the whole routine.

I must have danced at every amateur night in Harlem. I did the Odeon Theatre on 145th Street, the Lafayette Theatre on Seventh Avenue between 131st and 132nd Streets. Every time there was an amateur night, Mama had me on that stage.

She made me a little pair of black shorts, and I had a white blouse with big sleeves. I'd sing a little song, then do a little jazz routine. I'd put a series of steps together. Each step had eight bars, and if I did four steps, that's thirty-two bars.

Thirty-two bars is a chorus in jazz. With that, I could go in any direction: Charleston, Black Bottom, Mess Around, Snake Hips, Suzy Q, Pickin' Cherries, Shim-Sham. Those were the steps everybody did. Jazz steps. I never won anything back then. I was just one of many little girls. There were others better than me, especially if they were singers.

My Dream

At one time, we lived on 140th Street, and the windows of our apartment faced the back door of the Savoy Ballroom.

The Savoy was on the second floor of a two-story building that sprawled across an entire city block between 140th and 141st Streets on Lenox Avenue. It had a giant marquee with black, bold, block letters. On the street level were a beauty shop, a barbershop, a furniture store, and a bar on the corner. The sidewalks were always bustling, echoing at times with the cackling gossip of the ladies in the beauty shop and the raucous laughter of the men getting their hair cut next door.

The Savoy Ballroom was a place where blacks and whites were able to mingle and dance together. The actress Lana Turner had nicknamed the Savoy the "Home of Happy Feet," and everyone who was anyone, black and white, went there.

In the summer, when windows were open, my sister and

I liked to sit on the fire escape and watch the silhouettes of the dancers through the curtains of the Savoy. We could hardly wait for the music of the big bands to start. We could listen to the greatest orchestras in the world from our living room. And every time I got a chance, I'd dance. I loved to dance. I felt born to be a dancer. I'd make up dance routines and call out to my mother, "Look at me! Look at me!" I'd shimmy and turn a fast two-step, imitating the dancers I saw. Dancing was in my blood.

Twist Mouth's New Step

On Sundays after church, I was part of a group of kids who ran over to the Savoy just as the music was going to start. There was a four o'clock matinee, and the music just seemed to swing out onto the street. I loved to "cut up," dancing the Charleston on the sidewalk for tips and "eyeballing" the people as they passed by. Sometimes we had Charleston contests on the street, and people threw money at me. I'd make some pennies, a nickel, a dime, sometimes twenty-five cents. That was a lot of money.

Every week when Twist Mouth George arrived, everyone crowded around him. Twist Mouth was the best. He had added a new step to our way of dancing just about the time Charles Lindbergh left New York on the first solo flight across the Atlantic, on May 20, 1927. On the front page of the daily papers was the headline LINDY'S HOP! And that gave Shorty Snowden, another dancer at the Savoy, the idea to call this new style of dance the Lindy Hop.

Twist Mouth would take his partner into a swing step. And while he kept the two-step going, he took her and pushed her away from him. She stepped out, then returned with a twist step, holding her finger in the air. Everybody had been doing the Charleston, but once they saw Twist Mouth do the "breakaway," everything changed.

BIG GEORGE

I just loved to see Twist Mouth George, but I was never able to get too close. I was usually chased away by Big George, the doorman of the Savoy. It was Big George's job to decide who went into the Savoy.

"Hey, you!" Big George would warn, shooing me away. I'd scurry off, but when he wasn't looking, I'd inch my way back, one dance step at a time.

Big George was from New Orleans. His belt buckle was studded with diamond initials, he had diamond studs down the front of his tuxedo shirt, and he wore a big diamond ring on his pinky finger. He sat next to a bouncer at the front door.

Seemed to me, everybody who went into the Savoy went in dancing. I said to myself, "One day I will dance in that famous ballroom." The Savoy was the one place I wanted to be more than any other in the world.

Hey, Kid

On Easter Sunday when I was twelve, the Savoy was holding a "best-dressed couple" contest in the Easter parade. I had a new outfit, a lilac organdy dress and a tan coat that draped just below my knees. I was wearing my first pair of stockings and a new pair of black patent-leather shoes.

After church, as usual, I ran over to the Savoy to dance for tips with my friends. I was doing the Lindy Hop, watching the couples go in. I was there about fifteen or twenty minutes when I heard someone call out, "Hey, kid!"

I turned, and it was Twist Mouth George. "Me?"

"Yeah, you, kid, come here," he said.

I was flabbergasted, and as I moved in Twist Mouth's direction, he smiled his lopsided smile. He had had a stroke and it left him with a misshapen face, but he was still handsome. He always wore the best of suits, and on this Easter Sunday, he was dressed all in white, from head to toe—a suit, shoes, tie, and vest. He was about six feet tall and had the longest pair of legs I had ever seen. His hat was cocked to the twisted side of his face, and a gold chain swooped from his vest to his pants pocket.

"Listen, kid," he said. "You look like a good dancer. How would you like to dance with me?"

I stuttered, "You . . . you mean . . ."

"This afternoon, here at the Easter matinee," he said. "Would you like to do it?"

I nodded. I didn't know what to say. He patted my hand to reassure me, and said, "Wait here. I'll be right back." He went over to Big George, the doorman, and waved me toward him.

Big George rolled his eyes, making it clear that he recognized me, but he didn't say a word.

THE BALLROOM SWIRLS AROUND ME

Twist Mouth took my hand, and I had to run to keep up with him. There were two staircases that led up to the ballroom, and on the second floor the glass doors were open. Inside, it was a paradise of soft-tone lighting. Everything was bathed in blue and green and red. On the walls were mural-size drawings of dancers in exaggerated poses and movements. The ballroom swirled around me. I was breathless trying to take it all in.

The announcer declared, "Twist Mouth George and his new partner!"

"Just follow me," Twist Mouth whispered. "Don't worry— you'll be okay."

I placed my left hand confidently on his shoulder, and he slid my right hand into his sleek fingers. As we made our first swing-out, he grasped me around my waist and whirled me out into the middle of the dance floor. I was in rapture. I closed my eyes and my face tingled.

I followed Twist Mouth's lead as he took me into another swing step. Then he did a regular two-step, pulling me toward him and pushing me away. I stepped out and broke away with my own twist step, my hand sweeping through the air like I was flying. My feet hardly touched the ground.

I was actually doing what I had seen the other dancers do when I leaned on the edge of the fire escape and watched. My body was filled with an exquisite rhythm, and the pulse of each of my steps matched his.

The music had a brassy swing sound and a driving beat. The bandleader was the clarinetist Fess Williams, who had a top hat and sequined lapels. He strutted up and down the bandstand, conducting his fourteen-piece Royal Flush Orchestra.

As Twist Mouth George and I danced across the long mahogany floor, the people sitting around us roared. Then Twist Mouth clasped one of my hands in his, and with his other hand, he held my waist and spun me around. My body swooped into his and my legs stretched out behind him in a grand finale. Everyone was on their feet, clapping and shouting, "Bravo!"

Twist Mouth hoisted me onto his shoulders and paraded me around the floor. He carried me all the way to the door, put me down, thanked me, bussed me on the cheek with a little kiss, and led me out of the ballroom.

"Whee!" I had danced in the world's most famous ballroom with the world's most famous dancer: Twist Mouth George! I danced all the way home.

THE APOLLO THEATER

As a teenager, I started going to the Renaissance Ballroom to dance with my friends. We called it the Renny, and they had dances every Sunday from three in the afternoon to nine at night. I was there every week. My dance partner was Sonny Ashby.

One day, one of our friends said to us, "Why don't y'all sign up for the contest at the Apollo?"

The Apollo Theater was going to have a Lindy Hop contest. They were looking for dancers. Whoever won the contest at the Apollo would have a chance to go up against the white dancers from the Roseland Ballroom. So Sonny and I entered, not really expecting to win.

We had heard that Herbert White, otherwise known as

Whitey, was going to enter his dancers from the Savoy Ballroom. He was the dance master at the Savoy. He choreographed, designed, prodded, cajoled, produced, and directed all the dancing that was presented there. He was the original stage mother, the almighty guru of the dance world of swing, the Balanchine of the Lindy Hoppers, the man who made the Lindy Hop respectable and accepted by the world as an art form.

Whitey was easy to recognize. He had a stocky frame, a well-developed body, and a two-inch white streak that parted his hair in the center. He had brown eyes that crinkled at the edges and a complexion like a Hawaiian tan. He had a full bottom lip that trembled when he was displeased or blossomed into a wide grin when he was happy. He was streetwise and young people–wise.

Well, on the night of the contest, Sonny and I were like two odd outsiders, standing on the sidelines. Here were the top dancers from the Savoy Ballroom, and this was the first time we had ever seen them. The theater was packed to the rafters. No one even noticed us. We hadn't realized what we were up against.

The emcee opened the contest with a shout. When it was our turn to dance, the audience went wild. Being teenagers gave us an up with the audience. Sonny and I walked off with first prize!

The morning after the contest at the Apollo, as I was getting ready to go to school, there was a knock on the door. I asked who was there but couldn't really understand what they were saying. So I opened the door. And there stood Herbert White with two other men flanking him. I was to learn later that this was Whitey's form of intimidation. Of course, he was always charming and smiling. He said, "I saw you dance last night, and you were very good."

I invited him in, and I called out to Mama, "It's Mr. White from the Savoy Ballroom, and he wants to talk to me about the show."

"Don't take too long," Mama said. "You can't be late for school."

"Okay, I don't think it will take too long." I turned toward Whitey. "Right?"

"No, of course not," he whispered back. "As I was saying, I think you are a very good dancer, and I would like you to come to the Savoy and dance with our dancers. After last night, I'd rather you be with us instead of going up against us. Would you like to dance with us at the Savoy?"

"Would I? I'd love it . . . really," I replied.

"Well, I'd like for you to come to the ballroom this Saturday."

My First Paying Job

I loved dancing at the Savoy, but it didn't pay anything. At that time, Whitey was just looking for dancers to compete in the dance contests on Saturday nights. I was underage and needed permission to go into the Savoy. But I was also looking around, following the other dancers to the other dance halls in Harlem.

Leonard Reed was rehearsing a show at a place called the Utopia. I was standing outside, looking at his dancers. I knew I could do the routines better than they could.

Sure enough, he came out of a rehearsal red in the face and slammed the door. My two girlfriends and I stood there, frozen. He asked me, "Can you dance?"

"Yeah!" I told him.

"Well," he said, "do a time step." I did a time step, and he said, "Get in there and learn that routine." It was as simple as that. That was my first show, my first real paying job. I was fifteen years old.

I don't even remember the name of that show, but we went to Glens Falls, New York, and that's where the show opened. I was in the chorus line. There were about twelve girls. But my role lasted only two days, because the truant officer came and got me. I had left school, and Mama had said, "If they come for you, I'm going to tell them where you are." And that's what she did. See, they thought I had run off with a man, but I had just gone off to dance. They came and got me. The producer shouted, "What!" I was using makeup and he thought I was eighteen. When he found out I was only fifteen, he fired me.

The Harlem Race Riot

Mama came up by bus to take me home. When I got to Harlem, I couldn't believe it. In just a few days, things had changed dramatically. There were mounted police in front of every store. It was the aftermath of the Harlem race riot of March 19, 1935. A ten-year-old Puerto Rican boy had been caught shoplifting by a white storeowner on 125th Street. Rumors spread that the boy had been beaten and maybe killed. People were furious. Harlem erupted. People threw rocks. Stores were looted. Grocery stores were emptied. By the time it calmed down, Harlem was a mess and the Savoy Ballroom was closed, all its first-floor windows broken.

The riot was a wake-up call for the city of New York. Mayor Fiorello La Guardia put together a group of politicians, including Adam Clayton Powell Jr., to figure out what needed to be done. All the stores were white-owned, and blacks weren't even being employed in the places in which they spent what little money they had. It was the Great Depression. People were so poor. My mother and just about everyone else in Harlem were struggling to get jobs.

I was young. I didn't understand the politics or what it all meant. All I could think about was the one thing that really mattered to me. I was starting my career in dance, and dancing was free. The hottest dance in the country was the Lindy, and I was good at it. My one thought was: When is the Savoy going to open again? And it wasn't long before it did.

THE HARVEST MOON BALL

When Whitey told us about the Harvest Moon Ball, we were all ears. We just sat there in a corner of the Savoy and listened. The *New York Daily News* had come up with an idea to boost the city's tattered morale. They were going to sponsor the Harvest Moon Ball, a contest that would bring together the best dancers from all five boroughs.

It sure sounded exciting. All the kids began jabbering at once. Whitey wanted the Lindy Hop crown for the Savoy. He wanted us to start training real hard. We were to select the partners we wanted, work out our routines, and focus on winning the contest. It was a real pep talk, and Whitey fired us up.

The Harvest Moon Ball was hailed as the world's greatest contest for ballroom dancing. It was the Olympics of the dance world. It would include the waltz, tango, rumba, fox trot, and the Lindy Hop.

Contests were held in each of the five boroughs, and the winners were to compete in the grand finals to determine the overall champions. Preparing for the Harvest Moon Ball consumed all our time. We were all a little apprehensive about it. Here, for the first time, we were going to be judged by people other than the audience. We had to dance according to the rules the dancing committee set down for us. It bothered us to no end, because we had no real point of reference. We were being asked to do something that had never been done before. That's the way it was. It was a new way of dancing a contest. There was going to be a point system, with points for grace, execution, originality, and appearance.

The Semifinals

On the night of the semifinals, the Savoy was packed. The entire staff wore tuxedos and lavish gowns. All of the other dance teams were very elegant. The men wore white ties and tails, and the ladies had their beautiful ball gowns. But the Lindy Hop dancers wore flat shoes with rubber soles to grip the floor, and our skirts were very short to facilitate better movement on the dance floor.

The Lindy Hoppers got to the ballroom early, so as not to get lost in the huge crowd that had gathered to see the contest. We assembled at the far end of the ballroom, the

140th Street side, to line up for the grand march. And when the music struck up, the grand march began. The audience and judges saw the contestants for the first time.

We were all so excited, and everything seemed to happen so fast. The grand march ended and the contest was under-way. Chick Webb's band played like never before, and the whole place was swinging. The house howled when the Lindy Hoppers took the floor. Instead of dancing one team at a time as usual, Whitey danced four teams at once. It was like a four-ring circus. The first swing-out was like madness. All the Lindy Hop teams were picked for the finals.

The next day the papers were full of the contests, and we all gathered at the Savoy to look at the pictures. There was no grumbling about more rehearsals. Anything Whitey wanted us to do, we did it. The finals were going to be held about a week later in the Central Park Mall. We were going to dance under the stars and the harvest moon.

DRAINED AND DISAPPOINTED

On the night of the finals, we were told to meet at the Savoy at 5:00 P.M. We were going to be taken to dinner and then driven to the park by bus. All of the contestants were white, except for those from the Savoy. We were all nervous, but we were smiling with excitement at the same time. Then, while we were eating dinner, we heard that the park was jammed and that the bus wasn't going to be able to enter. There were too many people, so they had to cancel the contest on that glorious night and reschedule it for a later date. We were taken back to the Savoy, and by then, we were all drained and disappointed.

Well, it was unclear when the contest finals were going to be held, and Mama had made arrangements for me to go to camp in Connecticut as a recipient of some wealthy woman's generosity. She had donated her property so that poor Harlem kids could have a couple weeks out of the city. I had gone every summer before, but this year was different. On August 23, I'll never forget, I was at camp and some of the older girls yelled out to me, "Hey, Norma! You're in the newspaper."

I ignored them, because I didn't believe them. So they came over and showed me. The headline read, DANCE THRILL AWAITS 18,500 AT GARDEN. That's right. The finals of the Harvest Moon Ball were going to be held at Madison Square Garden, and the article went on to talk about the Lindy Hoppers: "We don't remember all of the 82 couples individually, but we'll never forget a few of them. There's Norma Miller and Bill Hill as a starter. Norma and Bill are two of Harlem's favorites, a couple of youngsters who were both born with syncopation in their veins and a strutting in their nature."

As I read along, everyone started talking at once. "You gotta go back! They think you can win!"

There was no doubt about it: I had to go back.

MADISON SQUARE GARDEN

Mama had never really approved of the Lindy: she hoped I'd eventually pursue a more "respectable" dance career. She couldn't understand how I could ever make a living doing the Lindy. She thought I should be a ballerina, or even a chorus girl. But when she picked me up at camp, her smile told me she was proud of me. And I headed back to Harlem.

At the Savoy, Whitey greeted me with a kiss and said, "Hey, sweetie, glad you're back. I was wondering if you were going to make the big contest."

Every day we had more rehearsals. And finally, after about a week of going over our steps and more steps, we were ready.

"Tonight," he said, "you're going up against real competition. We've got to show them what the Lindy Hop is all about. We are the champs. Do you dig?"

"We dig!" we all said at once.

When we arrived at the Garden, we were led in line to the arena. Four teams would compete. As soon as one team finished, another would go up. We were going to be the last team in our group of four. We could hardly wait. The white Lindy Hoppers went first. They seemed so clumsy to us. Watching them made us mad. By the time it was our turn, we were ready to burst. The bandleader, Fletcher Henderson, raised his baton, and thus began the wildest dance exhibition that had ever been seen.

When the winners were announced, the house went wild. I jumped up when they called my name. Whitey was beaming. Billy joined me onstage. "We did it!" we shouted. We had won third prize. Frankie Manning and Freda Washington won second prize; Leon James and Edith Matthews were the champions. The Savoy Lindy Hoppers were the best.

We Travel to Europe as Champions

The promoters of the Harvest Moon Ball wanted the top two couples to go on tour in Europe. But Frankie couldn't, because he had a job. Then they asked Billy and me if we'd go, and we said yes.

Now, how was I going to find a way to get my mother to sign for me? I was only fifteen, and she'd have to give her consent. I decided I'd hit it head-on. As soon as I walked into the apartment, I said, "Mama, I got a chance to go to Europe. Can I go?"

My mother was lying in bed, half asleep. "Yeah," she said. "You wash that underwear I got out in the sink, and you can go to Europe."

So I washed the underwear, hung it all out, and said, "Mama, I did all the underwear. Can I go to Europe now?"

She said, "Yeah, you can go to Europe." And she went back to sleep. And that was all.

A month later, she gets the permission forms she's got to sign. And that's when it hit the fan. But Whitey calmed her down. He explained that we'd have a chaperon, and he assured her that I'd be okay.

So I did go to Europe at fifteen years old. That was in 1935. I came out of school at three o'clock one afternoon, and I was on a boat that night. We had been studying European history, and there I was on my way to Europe. There were just four of us. Leon and Edith, Billy and me. We were the Harvest Moon Ball Lindy Hop champions.

Mama came with me in a taxi to the boat pier. She came onboard, and after a while, fell asleep in the stateroom that I was to share with Edith. We had to wake her up because they were calling for visitors to leave the boat. She hurried out of the stateroom and got off just in time, and I waved to her from the deck.

That night I slept better than a baby. We were on the deck that some people might have called steerage. It may have been the cheapest way to travel, but it was a palace to me. Now I had my own bed. I had been sharing a bed with my sister since I was born.

The next morning, I went to breakfast and acted like I knew what I was doing. A waiter with a napkin over his arm served me a roll. I tried to cut it in half and slab it with butter. But it was hard on the outside, and it slipped out of my hand and popped up and hit the ceiling of the dining room. When it landed, it rolled and rolled, and looked like it wasn't going to stop. I was totally embarrassed. Everyone turned and looked at me. I was the youngest person there. Nobody said a word. It was unbearably quiet; the waiter came over as if nothing had happened and placed another roll on my plate. I never made *that* mistake again.

Seven Amazing Days

On the boat over, the SS *Berengaria,* we had to entertain both the first- and second-class passengers at dinnertime. We went from one dining room to another. We had to dance for our supper. But we had a rickety band, and for the first time in my life, I realized that a lot of people couldn't play our kind of music. That took a little getting used to.

At that time it took seven amazing days to go from New York to Dover, England. The waters were calm in October, and I never got seasick. When I stepped off that boat, I didn't know what to think, because there wasn't much there. It was just a port with lots of boats everywhere. We had to take a train to London, and that's when I really felt like I had made it to another country. The British trains were far superior to anything I had ever seen. They had a lot more woodwork, and even though we were in second class, it was very comfortable.

In London, we played the Piccadilly Theatre. That was our first exposure to an audience in a theater. We worked with the great Kentucky Singers. At that time, you had a lot of American acts in Europe.

When we got to Paris, I started overhearing conversations about racism. It was my introduction to what was really happening in America. It seemed like a lot of the black tap dancers who had been in Europe for a long time were complaining, saying they weren't going back to America because of the discrimination. I hadn't experienced firsthand what they were talking about, but I was beginning to understand.

I Start to Have Opinions

We were supposed to stay in Europe for two weeks. We were there for ten months. One show led to another. I was never lonely. We were working every day, meeting some of the biggest actors and dancers. Just about everywhere I looked there was something I had never seen before.

My mother raised hell. We got to Paris one time—I'll never forget. We walked in, and somebody said, "Who is Norma Miller?"

I said, "I am."

He said, "Write your mother!" My mother had called all over the world to find me. Like a kid, I'd neglected to write, so that's what I did: I started writing.

Before I went to Europe, I hadn't been interested in the news, but once I was there, I was exposed. Hitler had been just a name until I started hearing about what was happening, that people were being arrested and that anti-Semitism and racism had run amok. We were told we couldn't go to Berlin. Our manager and chaperon, Herb Gale, was Jewish, and we were black. That was the first time we heard about the rumblings of the war to come.

In Europe, I started to have opinions. Things formed in my head even if I didn't want them to. I realized that anti-Semitism in Europe was just as bad as racism in America. Jews in Europe were being persecuted like blacks in the South. But in spite of all that was going on around me, I began to believe that dancing could overpower the politics. It allowed me, a young black woman, to go to the forefront. Dancing did more for politics than all the politicians in the world. The Lindy Hop was the most profound dance to come out of America. I was doing something that I loved more than anything in the world, and I was being paid for it.

People loved dancing. So when I was in the world of dance, we were the kings and queens. I was willing to endure anything to keep dancing. I got a place to sleep, I got food, and I got to dance. To be able to take what I knew and do it for people who wanted to see it was more than anything I could ever ask for.

WHITEY'S LINDY HOPPERS

When we got back from Europe, Whitey made it clear to us that he wanted to be the man who made the Lindy Hop famous. When he saw a dancer with potential, he set about to get him or her for his dancing empire. Whitey wanted his dancers to be unattached. He preferred to choose your dancing partner. He didn't like dancers with bad habits. He wouldn't put up with a Lindy Hopper who was under the influence of alcohol or drugs. If any of us was caught doing something that did not fit the image of the ballroom, we were reported to Whitey. Whitey had friends everywhere, and if we did anything, he'd hear about it. His dancers had to be clean-cut, single, and with one thought: dancing. Sometimes those happy feet were sore feet—with blisters, especially after an evening of pounding on that floor. But we loved doing it, blisters and all.

Whitey knew how to motivate us, and he kept the floor

alive with dancers. He left nothing to chance when it came to good swing dancing. He would teach a guy how to swing his girl and how to control his swing. On any night at the ballroom, you could see Whitey among his dancers, coaching them, walking among them like a football coach on the sidelines, pacing up and down, leading the cheering section, and applauding whenever a dancer did some breathtaking step. With a nod or a gesture, Whitey would send a dancer out on the floor. You danced to his tune, and he pulled the strings. The dancers moved to his beat. With the best bands in the land, there was never any problem getting the results he sought. He was totally devoted to his dancers, as they were to him.

ETHEL WATERS COMES TO THE SAVOY

One afternoon, a few of us at the Savoy noticed Whitey sitting with the most handsome black woman I had ever seen. She was tall and statuesque, with burnt brown skin. I knew I was in the presence of a star. She was, by far, the most famous black woman entertainer in the world at that time: Miss Ethel Waters.

Whitey was talking to her very softly. We couldn't hear what they were saying, but whatever she said, Whitey was in full agreement, beaming like a lit-up Christmas tree.

Whitey called us over to introduce us, and the guys scrambled to be first in line. I could imagine the thoughts of all these vibrant young men, meeting a woman of such magnitude. I was sure they were going to fantasize about this moment for a very long time.

Miss Waters looked at us with piercing eyes, a real stare that made us feel a little intimidated. She was kind, but we felt like we were in the presence of royalty. She was an extraordinarily strong woman, overpowering in her presence. She carried herself with such dignity and appeared to be about six feet tall.

Ethel Waters was thinking about adding the Lindy Hop to her touring show. Well, she had come to the right place and met the right man. We were all sitting around, totally enthralled by her presence.

Whitey had us take to the floor and give her a personal audition. Boy, did we swing. When we finished dancing for her, she thanked us, then Whitey escorted her to the door. Whitey returned with the expression of a man completely captivated, hogtied, and branded by a real star. Ethel Waters was going to take the Lindy Hoppers on tour!

That evening Miss Waters came back with her escort, Archie Savage. Archie and I were old friends, and he was a good dancer. While Miss Waters danced with Frankie Manning, I danced with Archie.

Whitey knew he had found an important ally in Miss Waters, and that was important to the lifeblood of the Lindy Hop.

When Ethel Waters left on tour, it was a big extravaganza. She had the Eddie Mallory Orchestra, the Brown Sisters, and Derby Wilson. We played all the Paramount Theaters across the country. The dancers and the band traveled in a bus, and Miss Waters and her entourage were in two chauffeur-driven Lincolns behind us.

As a group of black entertainers traveling on the road in 1937, we never knew what we were going to run into. One time, we pulled into a White Castle burger stand and were told, "We don't serve Negroes here." One of our musicians shot back, "Well, we don't eat Negroes. Just serve us a burger!"

The restaurant did not give in. This was not unusual. Often when we would pull into a town for a break and a bite to eat, we would be redirected to a place that would serve us. Some of these places had designated "Negro" entrances.

We stayed in black boardinghouses across the country, many of which were named for African American women and stops on the Underground Railroad. There was the Sojourner Truth House, the Harriet Tubman House, the Phillis Wheatley House, and others. Everywhere we went we had curfews and chaperons. There was no fraternizing between the dancers after hours. Miss Waters watched us like a hawk. She paid Whitey, and he paid us.

A Day at the Races

During our engagement in Cleveland, Miss Waters called at the Phillis Wheatley House, where we were staying, and left instructions for us to meet her at a big department store downtown. When we got to the store, we were told to meet her in the coat department, where she had us all try on coats. And she bought one for each of us. There we were with the star, Miss Ethel Waters. How lucky could a group of kids be?

Well, as kind and compassionate as Miss Waters was, she also had a very short fuse. Many times, as soon as the curtain came down, she turned around and started screaming. She'd rant and rave about things she didn't like. And we learned not to get in her way. If she wasn't clowning with Whitey, it was someone or something else.

When we got to California, we attracted the attention of MGM Studios. That led to our first major motion picture, *A Day at the Races,* with the Marx Brothers. The movie had already been made when they saw us, but they weren't happy with the last scene. They made a deal with Whitey, brought us in, brought the whole cast of the movie back, and reshot that scene.

This was my first time on a movie set. We were a highly disciplined group, but when we were on break, I could hardly contain myself. I saw movie stars: Clark Gable walking down the street going to the commissary, William Powell, Margaret Sullavan. . . . We were used to being around stars. We were

delighted, but we weren't giddy. I never talked to anyone unless I was talked to first.

Once I was peeping into the French actor Charles Boyer's dressing room and he caught me looking at him, and he asked me to come in. He was putting on his toupee. I was embarrassed, but he said, "C'mon in." I told him I'd been to Paris, and asked him if he liked working in America. He said he liked Hollywood. I imagine the money must have been better.

Whitey had been looking for a chance to get us away from Miss Waters. The picture deal was it. He believed that she was trying to take us away from him, and the two of them battled just about everywhere we went.

I CAN BARELY WALK

By the time we finished our engagement in California, I was a wreck. I had been doing four shows a day, five on Saturdays— at noon, three, five, nine, and eleven o'clock. Every night when we finished, we went to the number-one nightclub in town and performed the Lindy Hop. That's how the Lindy got spread across the country. I usually didn't get to bed until two or three o'clock in the morning.

The stress had left me unable to eat, and the last couple of shows I could barely walk, though somehow I managed to dance. When we returned to New York in July of 1937, I weighed only eighty-seven pounds. I was seventeen years old and completely burned out. Mama put me in the hospital, where I was fed intravenously and very slowly nursed back to health. I was in the hospital for five months. I didn't feel that sick, but the doctors kept me in there for my own good. When I came out on my eighteenth birthday, I had gained twelve pounds. A nurse took me out in a wheelchair, and I heard someone say they didn't think I'd make it. I still had a little fever, but they let me out because it was my birthday. My aunt said to Mama, "I'm gonna get her better," and she gave me round-the-clock service. I had to drink orange juice with a raw egg every morning.

I never lost my passion for dancing. There was nothing else I could do. I never even thought for a second about anything else. I was a dancer.

I Start Dancing Again

In March of 1938, I started dancing again. I was thrilled to be back at the Savoy. Everybody was happy to see me. I was a bit out of shape, but at eighteen, I was able to spring back very fast. And it wasn't long before we had some new excitement. The legendary record producer John Hammond was bringing Benny Goodman's band to Harlem to challenge Chick Webb, the undisputed King of Swing. Mr. Hammond wanted to prove that a white band could swing as well as a black band.

When the big night came, the great Chick Webb said, "The kid's good, but he's still learning. Tonight he'll get his next lesson." Chick let go with both barrels, and the sets kept getting better and better. Both bands pulled out all the stops. We danced like we would never stop. The Savoy was swinging! For his finale, Goodman played what everyone had been waiting for: "Sing, Sing, Sing."

By the end of the evening, there was no doubt about it. There was no real winner. Both bands came away from that ballroom with a lot of respect for each other. The night was filled with winners. The people won and the ballroom won. Harlem loved Benny Goodman. And everyone loved the Lindy Hoppers.

THE TOAST OF THE TOWN

Ed Sullivan was going to be the emcee of the 1940 Harvest Moon Ball at Madison Square Garden, and the winners would go on to dance in his *Toast of the Town Revue* at Loews State Theatre.

This was my fourth Harvest Moon Ball, and I knew how hard it was to get ready. Dancing at a fast pace for three minutes takes conditioning, and we needed to build up our lung power. The last Harvest Moon Ball, we got so tired, our teeth felt like they were falling out. Our arms got limp, and our lungs felt like they were going to burst! This time, we were going to be better prepared. The rehearsals were grueling, but we managed to have a good time, and all the hard work paid off. Tops Lee and Wilda Crawford took first prize, Frankie Manning and Ann Johnson came in second, and Billy and I were third.

Ed Sullivan was so impressed by all the talent that he did something he'd never done before. He announced to the Garden crowd that he was taking the best dancers to his *Toast of the Town Revue:* all three winning teams! When we opened at Loews State Theatre, we proved him right. We were sensational.

Not long after our performance at the State Theatre, Whitey got a call from Hollywood that the comedy team of Ole Olsen and Chic Johnson was going to make a film of the Broadway hit *Hellzapoppin',* and that they wanted the Lindy Hoppers. We had performed with *Hellzapoppin'* before it went to Broadway. We were excited about being in the film.

But Whitey was going to have to deal with us on a different level this time. We were more mature than when we were in *A Day at the Races.* We had all argued with Whitey about money at one time or another, and now we made some demands. In addition to what we would earn from the movie, he would pay us a per diem, and he would cover our hotel bill.

We were going to travel in style, on a train—no car, no bus. Whitey would still get his commission, but we wanted our fair share.

HELLZAPOPPIN'

Leaving for Los Angeles, we took a train from New York to Chicago, where we picked up *El Capitan,* another train that had sleepers, all the way to California. When we boarded, we met the steward, and we told him we didn't need to have the beds folded up every day, because we were not going to get out of bed the whole trip. And that's exactly what we did. We only left the sleeping car to eat, and then we headed right back to bed.

In L.A., Olsen and Johnson gave us star treatment. We were driven around in a limo and introduced to all the stars and studio executives. We met our choreographer, Nick Castle, one of the best dance directors in Hollywood. He'd never done any work with the Lindy, but we weren't worried. He understood swing, and had just choreographed *Jump for Joy,* a show at the Mayan Theater, starring Duke Ellington. That night, he took us to see the show.

There was one performer that I noticed in particular. When he spoke, his voice seemed to fill the entire theater. I was mesmerized.

Well, the next night, after a long day of shooting, a bunch of us went to Club Alabam on Central Avenue. I sat at a table and watched as several of the *Jump for Joy* cast walked in. Who was with them but the man with the amazing voice! I wanted to walk over and introduce myself, but I decided to get his attention in another way. I grabbed Frankie and went out on the dance floor. I wanted to be sure he noticed me, and I really turned it on. I kept looking his way until we made eye contact. When the number was over and I sat back down, he approached me and asked if I'd like to dance,

"No thanks," I said. "It's been a long day. I need to sit out a few."

"I saw you dance just now, and you're very good. Are you here with anyone in particular?"

"No, not really. There's a bunch of us here."

He sat down and introduced himself. "I'm Roy Glenn. What's your name?"

I told him, and we started talking about the show, his career, my career. And after a while, it was time for my group to go. He asked where I was staying and if he could see me home. I agreed, and we took our time walking back to the hotel. There seemed to be so much to say, but finally I said, "Good night"—that is, after a good-night kiss and a promise to meet again at Club Alabam the next night. Here I was working in Hollywood, and I'd met a wonderful man. I'd never had that feeling before.

In a short time we grew very close. I couldn't stand the thought of leaving. He felt the same, and we decided that I should return to live in Los Angeles as soon as I could wrap up my business in New York.

WE TRAVEL TO RIO

When we got back to New York, Whitey told us that we were to open in Rio de Janeiro in two weeks. I was stunned. The rest of the group seemed delighted, but it didn't fit into my plans at all.

"Rio?" I asked. "I'm not going to Rio! I'm going back to L.A. The only reason I came back to New York was to get paid. Now I'm gone."

Whitey tried to talk, but my mind was made up. "I don't care what you say, Whitey. I can't go. I got plans, and I'm not gonna break them."

The rest of the group slipped away, leaving Whitey and me alone. He put his arm around my shoulders and said, "I already know why you're so upset. Now, what have I told you from the beginning, about getting involved with men? They're no good for your career. That's not for you, Norma. You're better than that."

I was fuming.

"Why are you so upset with me?" Whitey asked. "You

know I'm only telling you this because I care. You're like my own daughter, sweetie. I just can't see you throwing away your career over some man."

I could not say no to Whitey. I was just too confused. I couldn't argue any longer. "Okay, I'll go to Rio," I said, with the thought that after Rio, I'd go to L.A.

We left New York Harbor on a cold winter day, December 1, 1941. We didn't linger ondeck, but hurried below. We were looking forward to some rest.

On our second day out, Frankie surprised me with a birthday party in the dining room after dinner. It was my twenty-second birthday, and he had the captain get me a cake with candles and all. The entire dining room sang "Happy Birthday." It was wonderful.

We arrived in Rio on December 5, just in time for our opening on December 6 at the Casino de Urca. It was spectacular. This was Las Vegas before there was Las Vegas. There were two large orchestras that came up out of the pit. Once the music started, it never stopped. There were one hundred girl singers, and there was a great samba show. The dancers all had big feather plumes and incredible costumes covered with beads and sequins.

The next day we went sightseeing along the Rio Branco, the main shopping drag. That's when we saw the newspaper headlines announcing the bombing of Pearl Harbor. America was going to war.

Our engagement in Rio was meant to last six weeks, but by the time our contract was up, we couldn't sail home. The harbor was closed because it was filled with German U-boats. They were sinking everything coming out of Rio. We just continued working. We stayed ten months.

I Would Have Gotten Married, Maybe

By the time I got back to New York, the Savoy was different. Men were being taken away in the draft, going off to the war. The big bands were getting smaller. Mambo had come in, and it was a new era. Bebop put a nail in the coffin of swing dancing—Charlie Parker, Dizzy Gillespie, and Max Roach. The music didn't have a swing beat. They didn't want people to dance. They wanted them to listen.

I decided to go back to California to look for work. I knew that Whitey had tricked me. I was one of his best dancers, and he didn't want to lose me. Roy and I saw each other again, but my feelings had changed. We had been apart for a long time. I wanted to get on with my life. I stopped Lindy Hopping in 1942 and didn't Lindy Hop again until I produced a show called *Swingin' at the Savoy* at the Village Gate in New York in 1977.

In California I started putting together shows. I choreographed jazz dance. Jazz dancers can solo; the Lindy was a couples dance. I worked for two years producing dance shows at Club Alabam in Los Angeles. Then I went back to New York and started choreographing shows at Smalls' Paradise in Harlem.

I started my own dance company, the Norma Miller Dancers. I've raised at least fourteen kids; my dancers are my kids. So many dancers started with me when they were just teenagers. I had always felt I could go beyond the Lindy Hop. I began to create new dances, new steps. I went into comedy. In the 1970s, Redd Foxx brought me to California to work in his nightclub, and then I followed him to Las Vegas, where he was doing a comedy show. I ended up collaborating with him for about ten years.

All of my life I've had rehearsals during the day and shows at night. Being by myself is a blessing. There are too many things to do. I'm always choreographing new shows in my head.

I live alone, but I'm not lonely. In my family, all the women that came to this country were supposed to get married. I mean, there was no issue. You came to America, you looked for a husband. My mother and father met at a ballroom. I would have gotten married, maybe, about forty years ago or something, but I was always on the road somewhere. I said I would never look for a husband, and I never had to because I always worked. I love what I'm doing. I love being a dancer.

I'm a very religious person deep down. I feel it in my heart. I believe in people. The most important thing in life is to be honest. Try to live your life right the first time. Whenever you do something wrong, you have to go back and straighten it out before you can go forward. I've never had to look back and say, "I wish I hadn't done that."

Acknowledgments

I am deeply grateful to Norma Miller, whose memories inspired me to begin this book and whose encouragement guided my efforts to completion. Frankie Manning, whom I interviewed in Washington, D.C., in the fall of 2000, when he received a National Heritage Fellowship from the National Endowment for the Arts, suggested that I contact Norma for the first time. My wife, Kaleta Doolin, accompanied me on my travels to New York to meet with Norma and has shared her enthusiasm as my work on this book evolved. My son, Alex, and my daughter, Breea, have grown to appreciate Norma mainly through her stories and the distinct pleasure they bring each time they are told.

NORMA MILLER got her start as a professional dancer as a teenager in 1934, when she was invited to join Herbert "Whitey" White's swing dance troupe, Whitey's Lindy Hoppers. By the late 1930s, the Lindy Hoppers were internationally renowned. The onset of World War II brought an abrupt end to their touring, but Norma never stopped dancing or performing, and began teaching new generations of dancers. A swing dance revival blossomed in the 1980s and continues today, nurtured by Norma Miller and Frankie Manning, the last two surviving members of the original Whitey's Lindy Hoppers. In 2003, the National Endowment for the Arts honored Norma Miller with a National Heritage Fellowship, the highest form of federal recognition for folk and traditional artists in America. Norma Miller lives in Florida, where she continues to teach, choreograph, dance, and "swing, baby, swing!"

ALAN GOVENAR is a filmmaker, photographer, folklorist, and writer. In 1985, he founded Documentary Arts, Inc., a nonprofit organization dedicated to presenting new perspectives on different cultures. He has written numerous books, including *Meeting the Blues, Masters of Traditional Arts,* and *Osceola: Memories of a Sharecropper's Daughter,* winner of a *Boston Globe–Horn Book* Honor. Alan's friendship and conversations with Norma Miller began in 2001. Those conversations formed the foundation of this oral autobiography. Alan Govenar lives in Texas.

MARTIN FRENCH earned his BFA in illustration and design in 1983. His work has earned him numerous awards, including honors from *American Illustration, Communication Arts,* and *Print.* The Society of Illustrators has awarded him gold and bronze medals. His energized imagery can also be seen in *The Song Shoots Out of My Mouth: A Celebration of Music* by Jamie Adoff. Martin French lives in Oregon.